About This Book

Title: *Space Crew*

Step: 5

Word Count: 241

Skills in Focus: Long vowel u spelled oo and ew

Tricky Words: astronauts, count, down, work, experiment, Apollo, first, walk, people, science

Ideas For Using This Book

Before Reading:
- **Comprehension:** Look at the title and cover image together. Walk through the pictures in the book with readers and have them make predictions about what they might learn while reading. Help them make connections by asking what they already know about astronauts and space crews.
- **Accuracy:** Practice saying the tricky words listed on page 1.
- **Phonics:** Tell students they will read words with long vowel teams. Explain that *ew* and *oo* make the long vowel sound /u/. Have students look at the title of this book, *Space Crew*. Ask readers to point to the vowel pairing in the title. Help them practice blending the sounds in *crew*. Have students take a quick look through the first few pages of text to identify and decode additional words with long /u/ sounds spelled with *ew* and *oo*.

During Reading:
- Have readers point under each word as they read it.
- **Decoding:** If readers are stuck on a word, help them say each sound and blend the sounds together smoothly. Be sure to point out words with vowel teams as they appear.
- **Comprehension:** Invite readers to talk about new things they are learning about space crews while reading. What are they learning that they didn't know before?

After Reading:
Discuss the book. Some ideas for questions:
- Would you go to space if you had the opportunity? Why or why not?
- What else do you wonder about space, astronauts, and space crews?

Space Crew

Text by Marley Richmond

Reading Consultant
Deborah MacPhee, PhD
Professor, School of Teaching and Learning
Illinois State University

PICTURE WINDOW BOOKS
a capstone imprint

Rockets send crews to space.

There are four astronauts on this crew.

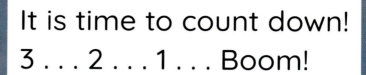

It is time to count down!
3 . . . 2 . . . 1 . . . Boom!

The rocket and its crew zoom off to space.

What Crews Do
The crew must eat, sleep, and work in space.

A space crew has lots of jobs.

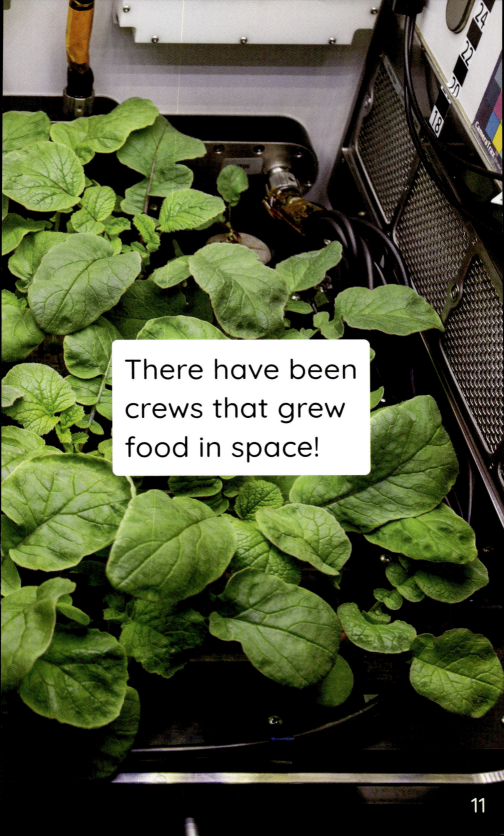

There have been crews that grew food in space!

But growing food is just one experiment a space crew can do.

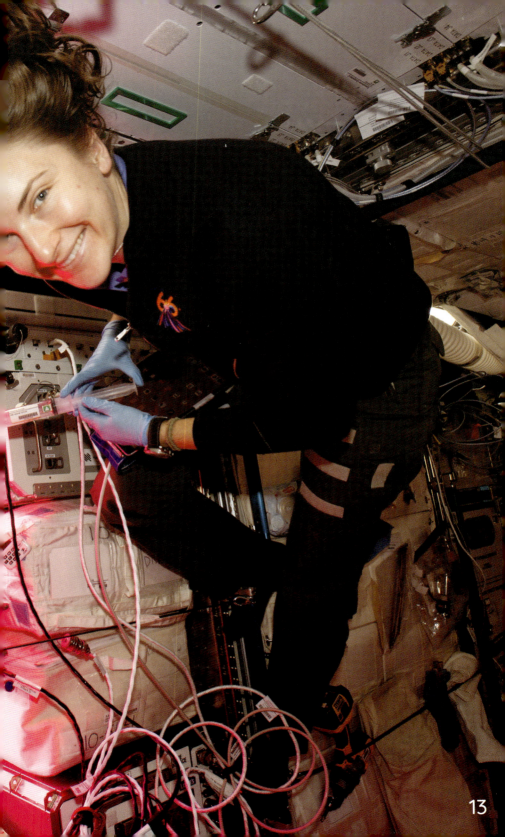

Crews do tests to see how water can be reused on a spaceship.

Crews do lots of other tests too.

The crew may need to fix the ship with tools.

Cool Space Crews

The crew on Apollo 8 was the first crew that flew around the Moon.

Apollo 11 had the first space crew to walk on the Moon.

There have been five space shuttles. They flew to space 135 times!

They had lots of cool people on their crews.

In 1983, the first Black man flew to space.

That year, the first American woman flew to space too.

Join the Crew
Not many people get to go to space.

To be on a crew, you must go to school for a long time and study math or science.

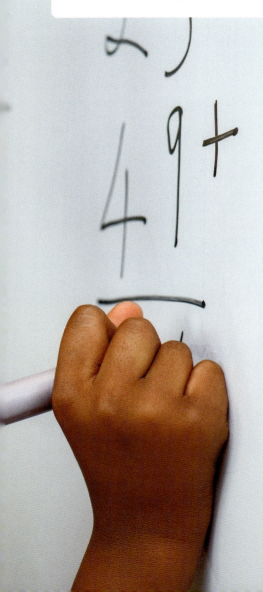

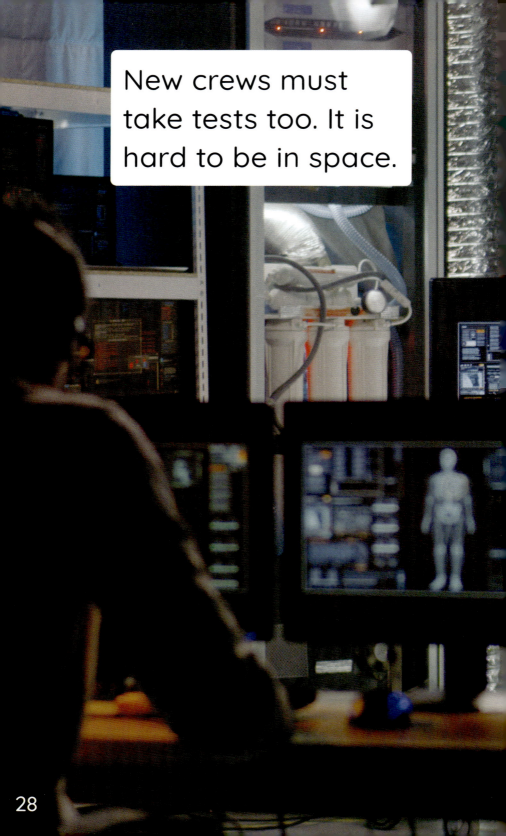

New crews must take tests too. It is hard to be in space.

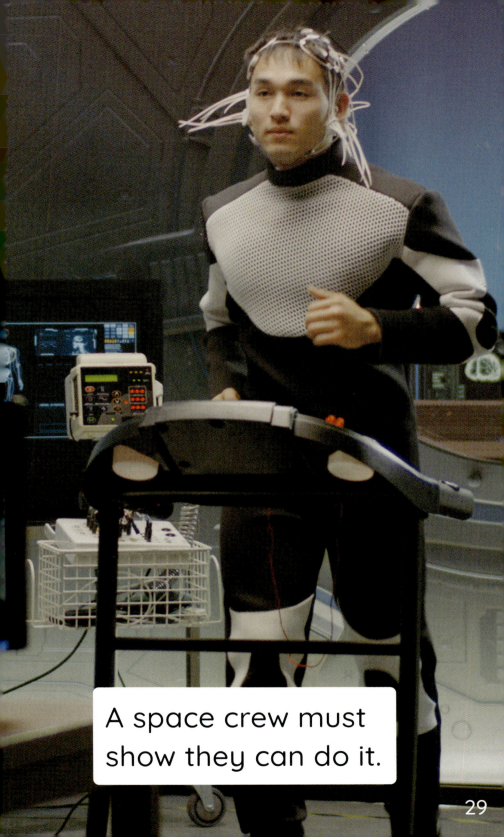

A space crew must show they can do it.

29

When a crew is ready, they shoot off to space!

More Ideas:

Phonics Activity

Writing with Vowel Teams:
Ask readers to pretend they are on a space crew. Ask them to write a letter to the crew's captain introducing themselves and explaining what they want to do in space. Readers might write about what they are excited to see in space or an experiment they want to try. Challenge readers to use vowel teams such as *ew* and *oo*.

Suggested words: crew, food, moon, school, new, too, shoot, cool, soon, tool, zoom, grew

Extended Learning Activity

Red Light, Green Light, Blast Off!
Ask readers to pretend they are on a space crew about to blast off in a rocket. They will play Red Light, Green Light as they make their way to space. To play, ask readers to line up along a starting line. When you say "green light," players will move toward the finish line. When you say "red light," everyone must stop. If players continue to move, they must return to the starting line. Once players make it across the finish line, ask them to write down one thing they are excited to do in space. Challenge readers to use words with *oo* or *ew* in their responses.

Published by Picture Window Books, an imprint of Capstone
1710 Roe Crest Drive, North Mankato, Minnesota 56003
capstonepub.com

Copyright © 2026 by Capstone.
All rights reserved. No part of this publication may be reproduced in whole or in part, or stored in a retrieval system, or transmitted in any form or by any means, electronic, mechanical, photocopying, recording, or otherwise, without written permission of the publisher.

Library of Congress Cataloging-in-Publication Data is available on the Library of Congress website.

ISBN: 9798875227219 (hardback)
ISBN: 9798875231063 (paperback)
ISBN: 9798875231049 (eBook PDF)

Image Credits: NASA: 8–9, 10–11; 12–13, 14, 18, 19, 20–21, 24, 25, Kim Shiflett, 5; Shutterstock: assistant, 22, Castleski, cover, Dima Zel, 4, Frame Stock Footage, 28–29, Gorodenkoff, 16–17, Ground Picture, 26–27, Hamara, 2–3, 32, Jose Antonio Perez, 30–31, New Africa, 15, NikoNomad, 1, 23, Oleg_Yakovlev, 6–7

Printed and bound in China. 6274